BODIES FROM THE ASH

A partial plaster cast was created from the remains of a person found at the House of the Sacerdos Amandus in Pompeii.

BODIES FROM THE ASH

JAMES M. DEEM

HOUGHTON MIFFLIN HARCOURT   BOSTON NEW YORK

FOR MATILDA W. WELTER

The text was set in Scala, ScalaSans, Neuland, and Pompeijana

Photo Credits:
Alinari/Art Resource, N.Y.: 9, 10, 14, 16, 19R, 21, 22, 30B
Alinari Archives/CORBIS: 19L
The Archeological Superintendency of Naples and Caserta: 6, 30T
The Archeological Superintendency of Pompeii: ii, 11, 15, 20L, 20R, 24, 26L, 27, 28L, 28R
Bettmann/CORBIS: vi, 29T
Bridgeman Art Library: 8
James M. Deem: 3R, 38, 43B
James M. Deem (as authorized by the Ministry of Cultural Heritage and Environment): 4T, 29B, 36, 39, 40, 41, 42L, 42R, 43T
Getty Images of North America: 37
Hulton Archive/Getty Images: 3L, 33
Jonathan Blair/CORBIS: 34, 35
Werner Forman Archives: 5, 23, 31, 32
Private collection: 4B, 12, 13, 17, 18, 25, 26R, 46, endpapers
Maps by Jerry Malone

Cover art: erupting volcano: Bettmann/CORBIS; gold border: Massimo Listri/CORBIS; painted background with columns: Mimmo Jodice/CORBIS;
child: Archaeological Superintendency of Pompeii; dog: private collection; urn: Archeological Superintendency of Naples and Caserta;
skull and hand with rings: Jonathan Blair/CORBIS; body on glass case: Alinari/Art Resource.
Back cover art: skeletons, face, and cast of child: Archaeological Superintendency of Pompeii.

The Library of Congress has cataloged the hardcover edition as follows:
Deem, James M.
Bodies from the ash/by James M. Deem
p. cm.
1. Pompeii (Extinct city)—Juvenile literature. 2. Vesuvius (Italy)—Eruption, 79—Juvenile literature.
3. Excavations (Archaeology)—Italy—Pompeii (Extinct city)—Juvenile literature. I. Title.
DG70.P7D386 2005
937'.7—dc22

ISBN: 978-0-618-47308-3 hardcover
ISBN: 978-1-328-74083-0 paperback

Manufactured in China
SCP 10 9 8 7 6 5 4
4500795975

CONTENTS

Bodies from the Ash

Mount Vesuvius had been dormant for 800 years before its massive eruption in AD 79. This eruption from 1925 was quite small in comparison.

CHAPTER ONE

AUGUST 24 AND 25, AD 79

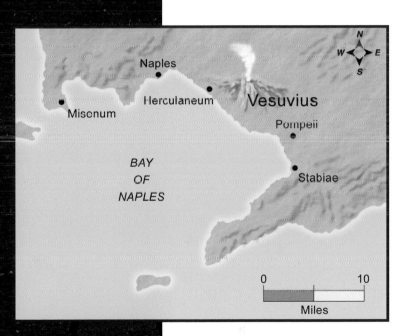

Inhabited by about 20,000 people, Pompeii, on the Bay of Naples, was one of the largest cities in the Roman Empire and had survived its share of wars and natural disasters.

On August 24, the last Tuesday that they would live in their town, the people of ancient Pompeii awoke to a typical hot summer's morning. Four days earlier, a series of small tremors had begun to shake the area, but people were not very concerned. The region had been subjected to so many earthquakes over the years that residents had grown accustomed to them.

What they didn't know is that the region's frequent earthquakes had been caused by nearby Mount Vesuvius. Roman writers had commented on the mountain's strange appearance; one had compared it to Mount Etna, an active volcano in Sicily. A writer named Strabo even concluded that Vesuvius had once "held craters of fire." But because Mount Vesuvius had been dormant, or sleeping, for more than eight hundred years, no one realized that it still had deadly power. What's more, no one understood that the region's frequent earthquakes were actually signs that Vesuvius was building up pressure and getting ready to erupt.

That morning, Vesuvius provided a clearer warning that an eruption was beginning. Between nine and ten o'clock, the volcano shot a small explosion of tiny ash particles into the air. To the residents of Pompeii, ten miles southeast of the volcano, this may have felt like a minor earthquake, but to the people living in the immediate vicinity of Vesuvius, it was terrifying. The ash streamed up and fell like fine mist on the eastern slope of Vesuvius. A woman named Rectina who lived at the foot of the volcano was so alarmed that she quickly sent a letter with a servant to Elder Pliny, the commander of Roman naval fleet stationed some eighteen miles away, urging him to rescue her.

People in Pompeii might have noticed the small cloud that morning and may have felt tremors, but they continued with their daily activities until early that afternoon. At one

ELDER PLINY'S LAST VOYAGE

That afternoon, Elder Pliny watched the eruption from his quarters in Misenum. When Rectina's message arrived, he realized how serious the situation was and ordered his fleet to rescue as many people as possible. By the time he reached Pompeii a few hours later, though, floating pumice and other volcanic debris blocked the harbor, forcing him to land in the nearby village of Stabiae. There, he met a friend who was preparing a ship to flee. In order to calm his friend, Elder Pliny bravely asked for a bath, followed by a meal. Then he went to bed but was awakened early in the morning when the eruption and the accompanying earthquakes worsened. Elder Pliny, his friend, and their companions hurried to their boats, but the sea was too choppy to set sail. Elder Pliny felt ill and asked for water. As the pyroclastic surges and flows approached Stabiae, the others fled, but Elder Pliny was unable to leave. Two days later his body was found on the beach.

Elder Pliny's story was recorded by his nephew, Younger Pliny, who remained behind in Misenum when his uncle sailed to Stabiae. He wrote two letters describing the eruption to a Roman historian named Tacitus. These letters have become the main source of historical information about the events of August 24 and 25. In fact, the explosive type of volcanic eruption demonstrated by Vesuvius in AD 79 is now called a *Plinian eruption*.

This cloud blasted from Vesuvius during its last eruption in 1944, but the cloud from the AD 79 eruption was much larger. Since AD 79, Vesuvius erupted thirty times before becoming dormant again.

The eruption cloud from Vesuvius was described by a writer named Younger Pliny as having the shape of an umbrella pine tree, much like the one pictured here. He wrote that the cloud "carried up to a very great height as if on a tree-trunk."

o'clock, eighty-one loaves of bread were baking in the ovens of the Modestus bakery, and vendors were selling fruit and other products in the *macellum*, or marketplace. The priests in the Temple of Isis were preparing to eat an afternoon meal of eggs and fish. It was then that Vesuvius finally awoke with a massive explosion.

An enormous pine-tree-shaped cloud of ash, pumice, and larger rock fragments blasted into the air. Within a half-hour, the cloud had risen over ten miles high, and winds had blown it toward the southeast—in the direction of Pompeii. The cloud blocked the sun and turned the sky over Pompeii to night. Then it began to release a deluge of ash, lightweight white pumice stones, and some larger, heavier volcanic rocks on Pompeii. At the same time, earth tremors continued to shake the town.

At first, most people would have taken shelter in their homes or other buildings. But as the volcanic fallout began to accumulate at the rate of five or six inches per hour and the

Most Pompeii streets were narrow and paved with stones. The larger stones helped pedestrians cross and prevented larger vehicles from traveling down them. They quickly filled with pumice and ash as the eruption progressed.

As the fallout continued, Pompeians made their way to one of the eight city gates, hoping to escape the deadly rain of Vesuvius. Pictured here is the Marina Gate on the southwest side of the town.

pumice grew to an inch in size, many decided to escape. Protecting themselves as best as they could from the falling stones, they headed down the narrow city streets, stepping on the accumulated fallout, toward one of the city gates. Some people used pillows and blankets tied to their heads; others shielded themselves with pans or even baskets. After reaching the gates, many took the coast road; others tried to escape by sea. But the buoyant pumice floated in the water, filling the harbor and making a seagoing escape more difficult. During this time, some were killed on their way out of the city, hit by larger rocks falling from the eruption cloud.

By five-thirty that afternoon, two feet of ash and stones had accumulated in the streets, on roofs, and in open areas such as the courtyards of houses and gardens. In fact, so much pumice had built up on roofs that some buildings began to collapse, especially when the loose pumice was shaken by strong earth tremors. Many Pompeians were crushed in their houses when the roofs caved in on them.

As the evening progressed, the raining pumice turned from white to gray and grew bigger, some pieces almost three inches in size. By midnight, first-story doors and windows were completely blocked by fallout. Anyone who had delayed escape would have had to use a second-floor window to reach the street and then walk atop five feet or more of collected stones and ash. Fires were burning on the slopes of Vesuvius. Lightning filled the sky around it, and the eruption cloud had risen almost twenty miles high. But no one in Pompeii would have been able to see this.

At about one o'clock on the morning of August 25, twelve hours after the first major explosion, the eruption shifted to its second—and deadlier—phase. Vesuvius was losing strength and its eruption cloud was beginning to weaken. As the cloud collapsed completely over the next seven hours, it would fall in six separate stages, each one producing a *pyroclastic surge and flow*. With each partial collapse, a surge of superhot gas and ash blew down the slopes of Vesuvius at speeds between 60 and 180 miles per hour and at temperatures ranging between 350 and 650 degrees Fahrenheit, each surge larger than the last, each one spreading farther. The surge cloud destroyed everything in its path, leaving behind a layer of ash. This was quickly followed by a very rapid pyroclastic flow of volcanic debris that covered the area like a hot avalanche. The flow itself was not lava (that is, a melted rock that would have moved slowly and burned every-thing it touched); rather, it was a mixture of rock fragments and gas that rolled over the ground at temperatures up to 400 degrees Fahrenheit. This combination of surge and flow is sometimes referred to as a *nuée ardente*, or glowing cloud; it is the most deadly type of volcanic activity because of its high temperature and speed.

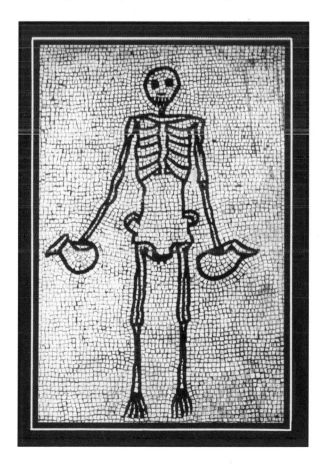

Skeleton images were frequently found in floor mosaics, wall paintings, and even on drinking cups in Pompeii. Such designs served as a reminder that life was short.

This lantern was recovered by archaeologists from a street in Pompeii. Someone carried it in a futile effort to escape the city.

The first and second surges in the early morning hours did not reach as far as Pompeii, but they did destroy other towns closer to Vesuvius. At about six-thirty, a third surge ended at the northern edge of Pompeii, destroying some of the walls surrounding the city and suffocating anyone who had taken shelter in any of the outlying buildings.

By morning, nine feet of pumice and other volcanic debris had accumulated, but the estimated two thousand people in and around Pompeii who had survived the night might have thought that they still had an opportunity to escape. By then, the rain of pumice had lessened so noticeably that many residents took to the streets, which were still darkened by the volcanic cloud, trying to get out of town. Many were carrying lanterns to help them see in the darkness.

But they were cut down around seven-thirty, when a fourth surge engulfed the city and the area beyond it, immediately killing everyone still alive, whether they were inside or out. Some fifteen minutes later, a fifth surge exploded through. Both of these surges deposited a layer of hot ash and a larger amount of pyroclastic flow.

Finally, at about eight o'clock that morning, a final surge—the largest and most violent—shook the area as the remainder of the volcanic cloud collapsed, crushing the top stories of buildings. Bricks, tiles, stones, and other debris were blown through the town. The last surge deposited two more feet of ash and debris on top of the town. But by then there was no one left alive to notice what had happened.

When the eruption ended, Pompeii was covered with more than twelve feet of volcanic debris. Only the very tops of a few ruined buildings were visible; most of the higher stories had been blown down during the pyroclastic surges.

In the days that followed, residents who returned hoping to find their city would have been lost in an unfamiliar landscape. Valleys were filled in; new hills had grown; and the course of the nearby river Sarno had changed. Even Vesuvius had a new look. The volcano's conelike top had collapsed, leaving a gaping crater.

And everywhere they would have looked, the landscape was blanketed by a ghostly covering of ash.

STAGES OF THE ERUPTION, AD 79

August 24

9:00–10:00 AM	Eruption begins with a small explosion and thin layer of ash
1:00 PM	First eruption phase begins: Massive explosion, emission of huge eruption cloud
1:30 PM	Fallout of ash, pumice, and other material begins to rain on Pompeii
5:30 PM	Accumulation of pumice on roofs causes buildings to begin collapsing

August 25

Midnight	Eruption cloud reaches about twenty miles in height
1:00 AM	Second eruption phase begins: Eruption cloud begins to collapse
1:00–2:00 AM	Surges 1 and 2 overwhelm Herculaneum, Oplontis, and Boscoreale
2:00–6:30 AM	Pumice fall decreases
6:30 AM	Surge 3 reaches Pompeii's town walls
7:30–7:45 AM	Surges 4 and 5 overwhelm Pompeii and neighboring cities
8:00 AM	Surge 6 adds two more feet of debris and ash

TIMING THE ERUPTION

Many people are curious how scientists and historians have been able to determine the stages of an eruption that happened such a long time ago. They have concluded, for example, that the eruption began about one o'clock because of information Younger Pliny gives in his first letter to Tacitus. They also deduced that the final surge occurred about eight o'clock the next morning, again because of information provided by Younger Pliny. With these two times, archaeologists and vulcanologists (that is, scientists who study volcanoes) have been able to create an approximate timeline by using information taken from archaeological excavations and studies of the fallout layers from the first eruption phase and of the pyroclastic deposits from the second eruption phase.

In 1865 the artist Edouard Sain painted an imaginary version of the excavations at Pompeii. In reality, slaves and convicts were often used to excavate the ruins during the early years that it was explored.

CHAPTER TWO

REDISCOVERING POMPEII

No one knows what happened to the residents of Pompeii who managed to escape, since no written record from any survivor of the town has ever been found. Some people may have left the area; others may have relocated to nearby towns unaffected by the tragedy. Some researchers believe that a few people returned and tunneled into the ruins, trying to salvage what they could, since tunnels have been found during excavations within the ruins. But no one tried to rebuild the city.

By the fourth century AD, some 220 years after Vesuvius erupted, Pompeii's name no longer appeared on maps. Instead, the area was called Civitas. The volcanic ash that buried the town became fertile soil, and farmers planted olive trees and grapevines there. Sometimes they would come across bricks and other building materials that poked out of the ground. On rare occasions, a farmer might even find a statue hidden in the undergrowth. In 1594 an attempt to build an underground canal brought workers tantalizingly close to the ancient city. They found pieces

A tourist poses on the hardened lava flow of Vesuvius around the year 1900. Although the AD 79 eruption did not produce any lava, other later eruptions did.

of marble, parts of painted walls, and statues. But no one realized that the discoveries might lead to the site of the long-buried town.

Pompeii and its secrets remained hidden for centuries. It was only after the town of Herculaneum, which was also buried by Vesuvius in AD 79, was discovered that excavators began digging for Pompeii. In 1709, a group of well diggers came across some beautiful marble. Since the prince in charge of the region was building a new villa nearby, he was told of the discovery. No one knew that the marble was part of a theater or that it was situated in the ancient town of Herculaneum. Instead, the prince ordered an excavation, hoping to find even more marble for his house. Seven years later, when the prince's opulent villa was completed, he ordered workers to stop digging. During that time, they had stripped the theater of its statues and marble façade, without even knowing what they had found.

This model depicts the theater in Herculaneum before early excavators looking for treasure plundered it.

In 1738, after the Bourbon king Charles III took control of the region, he was eager to find more buried treasures from the same site, so he hired a Spanish military engineer named Alcubierre. In short order, Alcubierre widened the entrance to the site, quickly discovering that the treasure was part of a theater. He also found an inscription that finally identified the location as Herculaneum. But in his haste to please Charles, Alcubierre essentially turned the site into a tunnel-filled coal mine. Soon, workers were hauling beautiful statues and other treasures out of the tunnels and sending them to the palace of Charles III.

After fourteen years, workers began to find fewer objects, but Alcubierre was not about to give up. Instead, he planned to try another site: the underground canal that had been attempted in the late 1500s. He hoped that it might lead to the ruins of Pompeii—and further favor from Charles III.

On March 30, 1748, a small crew of twenty-four men, twelve of them convicts, began work. Digging was easier at the canal site, but it was filled with areas of firedamp—that is, toxic gasses trapped in the layers being excavated. Every time a pocket of firedamp was exposed, the diggers would have to run away to escape breathing the poisonous gas, and their work could be interrupted for many days.

Twenty days later, the workers discovered something unexpected: the skeleton of a man who had died during the eruption. The excavation report for that day read only: "Found a skeleton and 18 coins." Although this was the first recorded sign of the human tragedy at Pompeii, Alcubierre was more interested in the coins than the man. A few days later, another entry read: "Nothing was found, and only ruined structures were uncovered." Eventually, he became so disappointed with the meager discoveries that he returned to the excavations at Herculaneum, leaving only a small crew to work at the canal site. No more than fifty men—some of them Algerian and Tunisian slaves, chained together in pairs—seemed to have been used at any time, even after the site was finally identified as Pompeii in 1763.

But Pompeii was about to get much more attention. In 1771 excavators made a dramatic find: a large, luxurious house, now called the Villa of Diomedes, complete with two skeletons near the garden. These skeletons were of much greater interest, thanks to the riches found with them. Next to one man, who held a key and wore a gold ring, was a hoard of coins wrapped in a cloth: ten gold, eighty-eight silver, and nine bronze. This turned out to be one of the largest collections of money found at Pompeii and certainly a dazzling find in 1771.

Early excavators were less interested in the discovery of skeletons than the coins or jewelry they may have carried during their attempted escape.

NAMING THE HOUSES

Most of the names given to Pompeian houses were not used when people lived in the town. Instead, they were usually invented by excavators and archaeologists. For example, the Villa of Diomedes was named not for its unknown owner but for the tomb of a man located outside the front entrance of the house. Other houses were named for objects or artwork discovered there during excavation.

This early photo shows the Villa of Diomedes after it was excavated. The crypto-porticus where twenty skeletons were found lies behind the pillars along the lower floor of the house.

The next year, as excavations of the house continued, workers discovered twenty more skeletons (eighteen adults and two children) piled together in a nearby underground room. The volcanic debris that had oozed into the room during the pyroclastic flows had hardened around the bodies and created imprints of the people, their clothing, and even their hair. Excavators studied the impressions and concluded that they had found a family and its servants. The woman of the house wore beautifully woven clothing and was adorned with a great deal of jewelry (multiple necklaces, armbands, bracelets, and rings). She carried a young boy in her arms. A young girl wearing golden jewelry accompanied her; as the fourth surge hit, she had covered her face with her clothing, gasping for breath.

The rest of the victims were dressed quite differently. Most wore canvas or cloth socks that were more like leggings; many had no shoes. The excavators concluded that they were slaves or servants. They also came to believe that the two skeletons found the previous year were the male head of the family, who carried the family's most valuable possessions, and another slave.

Word of this discovery and others traveled around the world. Pompeii and its Villa of Diomedes became part of the grand tour for wealthy American and English travelers. As a result, many tourists flocked to the ruins, not only to watch the excavators, but also to see the skeletons. They would wander through the ruins to encounter tableaux; that is, little scenes arranged by excavators that featured skeletons and objects found at the site. Two victims that fascinated early visitors to the site, according to the writer Jennifer Wallace, were found in the Gladiator's Barracks in 1766. These two men, either prisoners or gladiators, were said to have still been in shackles and chained to the wall when they died in the eruption. Excavators placed their skulls on shelves for all visitors to see.

Unfortunately, some tourists stole bones from the skeletons and other artifacts as souvenirs, since the large site was poorly guarded. It is not surprising, therefore, that of all the coins and jewelry found at the Villa of Diomedes, only two items have been preserved to this day: a necklace and a gemstone. The rest have disappeared without a trace.

Early visitors to Pompeii often saw tableaux, or staged scenes, in which skeletons or bodies were displayed. Here, an artist from the 1800s shows tourists coming across a skeleton in a house, which was arranged for their enjoyment by excavators.

By the middle of the nineteenth century, much had been discovered at Pompeii, but nothing prepared the world for the excitement caused by a new excavator named Giuseppe Fiorelli. Appointed in 1860, he made many important changes that helped preserve Pompeii. He understood that treasure-hunting excavators had ruined a great deal of historical and scientific information. He also realized that Pompeii had much to teach the world, if the excavations were thorough and carefully recorded.

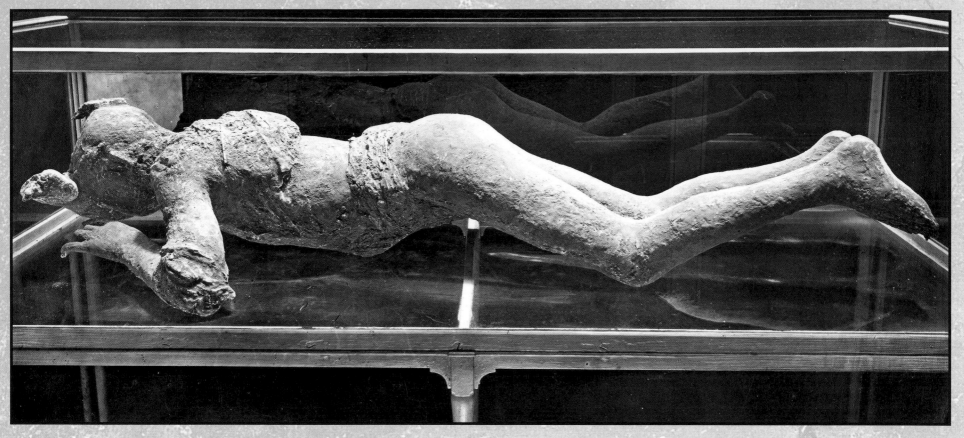

This woman's remains were discovered in 1875. Her plaster cast became so famous that it was photographed frequently, drawn by artists, and reproduced on postcards sold to tourists.

Three years later, on February 5, 1863, Fiorelli's workers came across some hollow areas in the ash that they were digging in along a lane soon to be called the Alley of the Skeletons. Peering inside the cavities, they could see bones lying at the bottom. They called Fiorelli, who was ready to take a revolutionary step in the study of human remains at Pompeii. He instructed workers to, rather than remove the skeletons, fill the hollow spaces with plaster. He had used a similar technique when workers had uncovered spaces where doors, shutters, furniture, and even tree stumps had once stood before decaying over time. When the plaster had hardened in a few days' time and the outer layer of volcanic debris was chipped

CHAPTER THREE

The Plaster Bodies of Pompeii

From then on, whenever workers discovered a skeleton in the ash, they attempted to recapture the last moment of another victim. Not every person left a hollow space, but many did. Most of the casts they created were chilling, and provided details about not only the person's appearance but his last living moment.

The victims of Vesuvius in Pompeii would not have died an instantaneous death. According to the scientist Paul Wilkinson, they might have had a chance to take three breaths of hot gas and ash before they stopped breathing. But those three breaths, in which they essentially lined their lungs and esophagus with superheated ash, caused them to suffocate. During that brief time, many writhed in agony, as shown by the plaster casts. Surprisingly, some others look as if they simply fell asleep.

The plaster casts amazed the world. Photographers took many photos of them and sold them to tourists as dramatic souvenirs of a visit to the ruins. Like the skeletons before them, some of the plaster bodies

The antiquarium at Pompeii exhibited plaster casts and other artifacts found in the ruins. It was badly damaged by Allied bombing in World War II and remains closed today.

Vendors sold souvenir albums of photographs that contained images of Pompeii and the plaster bodies.

were placed in the ruins so that visitors could experience the sensation of seeing the victim in the location near where he or she had died.

Eventually, an antiquarium, or museum, was started at Pompeii, which displayed many of the casts and some of the artifacts that had been found there. One writer commented that the bodies placed there "are reproduced just as they were when death struck them; some wrestling against it in despair, others yielding without resistance. It is a striking sight, and one of the greatest curiosities of Pompeii."

As word spread about Fiorelli's creative technique, more and more people journeyed to Pompeii to see the plaster people and the ruins of a city that provided a snapshot of life during the Roman Empire. While they were there, many also made the ascent to the top of Mount Vesuvius despite its periodic deadly eruptions. The trip for early visitors was lengthy; they either hiked to the crater or were carried in a sedan chair. Eventually, so many tourists came to Vesuvius that a funicular was built. When it was damaged by an eruption, a chairlift took its place until it was shut down in 1984.

Tourists may have been amazed at everything that Pompeii had to offer, but scientists were still puzzled. They wanted to know why some bodies left hollow spaces in the volcanic material, while others became only skeletons.

Visiting the top of Mount Vesuvius was so popular that a funicular was opened in 1880 to make the climb easier for tourists. But a subsequent eruption in 1944 damaged the railway so badly that it was never used again.

This person was found in the large palestra, or gymnasium. After the plaster dried, the outer layer of volcanic debris was chipped away until the plaster cast remained.

Afterward, a technician often fine-tuned the cast by patching missing parts and correcting other defects in the plaster.

Over the years, they studied the debris that came from Vesuvius, pinpointed the locations where people were found, and analyzed the skeletons and plaster casts themselves. In the end, they concluded that the time and place that a person died during the eruption determined whether the person's body left a cavity in the volcanic debris.

Time of death. Scientists found that a person who died during the surge of hot gas and ash after dawn on the second day of the eruption was more likely to create a cavity in the volcanic material than someone who died the first day during the pumice fall. For example, a woman fleeing the city who died in the fourth pyroclastic surge was immediately covered with hot ash that molded itself to her skin and clothing. Next her body was covered with a layer of volcanic debris in the pyroclastic flow that followed. The last two surges and flows buried her completely. Soon, the volcanic matter surrounding her body began to harden as it cooled. Eventually, the woman's body began to decay inside the hardened deposit, leaving behind a hollowed space and a skeleton where her body had once lain.

This wouldn't have happened, however, if the woman had died as she attempted to leave town on the first day of the eruption. She would have been covered mostly with pumice, rather than ash. Because the pumice was granular and did not stick to the body like ash, it would not have created a hardened mold of the woman. Her body would have become a skeleton without a well-defined cavity around it. For this reason, no plaster casts have been made from people found only in layers of pumice.

Location of death. Scientists also discovered that the place a person died also determined whether a cavity would be formed. For example, a man who died inside his house, either on the first or second day, would not have been covered with ash. Instead, he was surrounded by pumice that fell through windows, doors, and courtyards, or by building material from collapsed roofs and walls. However, if the man had died in an area where the hot ash from the final surges could coat his body, a hollow cavity was formed as his body decayed.

In studying the plaster casts, archaeologists have also learned something else. Because of the circumstances under which the victims died, not all of the hollow spaces that the decaying bodies created could produce an entire person. Some people, for example, were not completely covered by hot ash. As a result, only part of their body could be recreated in plaster. Others may have been completely formed, but during the centuries that followed the eruption, earthquakes may have damaged the cavities as the ground shifted and collapsed.

For these reasons, some of the plaster bodies are strangely incomplete, while others look like odd sculptures. Sometimes workers even used a bit of artistic license after they chipped off the volcanic ash and cleaned up the cast. When facial features were missing on incomplete casts, workers occasionally added them, sculpting a nose or ears and carving a mouth and eyes.

Sometimes only a partial mold was created.

21

The unusual plaster cast of this man may have been a result of subsequent earthquakes that caused part of the hollow space around the man's remains to collapse.

COUNTING THE DEAD

Since 1748 when Alcubierre's workers found the first skeleton, approximately 1,150 human remains have been recovered at Pompeii. Some 394 skeletons were located in the pumice deposits from the first day, most of them inside buildings. About 655 were found in the pyroclastic flows of the second day. These were almost evenly divided between those killed on roads or other outdoor spaces and those who died in buildings. The skeletal remains of about 100 other people have also been found, but they were simply bits of bones that scientists cannot place in either group.

Workers wait for the plaster to dry on the cast of a body found at the House of the Cryptoporticus.

CHAPTER FOUR

LIVES FROM THE ASH

Ten people died in the garden of the House of the Cryptoporticus.

The plaster casts and skeletons of the victims of Vesuvius have become windows to what Pompeii life was like in AD 79. Through their studies, archaeologists and other scientists have tried to describe the life and death of the person. Although the stories they told were based on fact, writers would often add a bit of creative imagination to the retelling. For example, when the skeleton of a man was found in a sheltered area of the Herculaneum Gate in 1763, some writers assumed that he was a loyal sentry who guarded the gate until the eruption buried him alive. After all, it made for a dramatic story. The truth, however, is that a man simply took shelter near the gate, where the pyroclastic surges and flows killed him.

Here are a few of the people whose remains were found at Pompeii and the stories that archaeologists have told about them:

This man was killed in the garden at the House of the Cryptoporticus.

This postcard shows the cryptoporticus where wine jugs were stored. After the house was excavated, the plaster casts of the victims killed there were exhibited in the cryptoporticus.

House of the Cryptoporticus

A group of skeletons was unearthed in what is now called the House of the Cryptoporticus. Although a cryptoporticus is an underground passage of a villa meant to provide shade and a space for walking, the cryptoporticus of this house had been altered to use for storing wine jugs, called amphorae. The house itself, which was still being repaired after an earthquake in AD 62, was a restaurant with a triclinium, or dining room with three couches, in this case for warm-weather banquets.

In 1914, excavators uncovered ten victims, most in the garden. These people may have lived in the house; some may also have been customers of the restaurant. On the first day of the eruption, they took shelter in the cryptoporticus below the restaurant. By the next morning, they decided to make a run for safety, across the garden in the back of the house. They held tiles above their heads to protect themselves from the falling pumice. As the fourth surge overtook them, they quickly suffocated.

Of the ten skeletons, archaeologists were able to turn four into plaster casts. Two appear to be a mother and her teenage daughter, who were embracing each other in their last moment. Another victim was a slave. His plaster cast shows that he was trying to release his ankles from the large iron bonds that shackled them. Researchers report that he was the third slave found at Pompeii with iron rings around his ankles. The fourth cast was another man, who carried two silver goblets and a simpulum, a silver ladle used in religious ceremonies.

What surprised archaeologists about this man was his collection of silver, which was not common outside of wealthy homes. Little silver has been found next to the fleeing victims of Pompeii. Could he have been a priest from a temple where the simpulum was used? Or could he have been a thief? No one will ever know.

A female skeleton found in the House of the Golden Bracelet wore a heavy bracelet of unusual design.

This cast of a child was one of the four made at the House of the Golden Bracelet.

House of the Golden Bracelet

One of the largest and most beautiful houses in Pompeii, the House of the Golden Bracelet was both a hotel and restaurant, built on three levels. The top floor of the building was typical of Roman homes', with an atrium surrounded by many rooms. The middle floor was the most lavish, with many reception rooms, multiple dining rooms, and a bathing area. The lower floor contained a beautifully decorated dining room that led to a large garden. Excavators named the house after a beautiful solid-gold bracelet with a two-headed snake that they discovered on the arm of one skeleton inside the house; the bracelet weighed a hefty one and one-third pounds.

As excavators uncovered the house in 1974, they found cavities containing four skeletons at the bottom of the staircase that led to the garden. Archaeologists believe that these people were members of a young family, most likely killed the second morning of the eruption when the stairs to the second floor collapsed. No one knows if they were the owners of the house or merely residents there, but near them, scattered over the lower floor, were jewels and more than two hundred gold and silver coins. Whoever they were, they had a considerable fortune with them.

Garden of the Fugitives

Sometime after the third surge early on August 25, a group of thirteen people banded together in their attempt to flee the city. They headed for the Nucerian Gate, on the south side of Pompeii. Although they had tried to leave during what they thought was a good time, they were caught in the fourth surge and died, overcome by the hot gas and ash.

The cavities that provided the molds of their bodies were discovered in 1961 in a vineyard area near the Nucerian Gate that is now named the Garden of the Fugitives. According to Amedeo Maiuri, who directed the excavations at the time of their discovery, they are the largest and best preserved group of people to have been found. Their group included seven adults and six children—what Maiuri thought was three separate families, though this is hard to prove.

The person who led the way, according to Maiuri, was a servant or slave, who carried a large bag stuffed with food. Two young boys followed him. One was using a pan to protect his head from the falling ash and pumice. At the end of the group was a man that Maiuri called a merchant.

As the surge overtook the group, each reacted to his or her final moment in a different way. The man in front seemed to have keeled over, his bag still slung over his right shoulder. The two young boys fell on their backs, looking up toward the sky for the last time. And the merchant tried to lift himself up, his right arm pushing against the ash.

Workers under the direction of archaeologist Amedeo Maiuri created thirteen plaster casts at the site now known as the Garden of the Fugitives.

Maiuri's merchant struggles to push himself up before being overwhelmed by the fourth surge.

Decorated with a relief of olives, this cantharus, or drinking cup, was part of the silver hoard discovered in the House of Menander.

This group of people attempted to climb the staircase in the House of Menander to make their escape.

FACING: *This chained guard dog in the House of Orpheus was suffocated by the ashfall.*

House of Menander

The large house of a wealthy family, the House of Menander was being remodeled at the time of the eruption. Furniture had been emptied from some rooms and piled in others. The owner of the house, Quintus Poppeus, had moved out during the renovation and left a freedman, or former slave, in charge. Because the house was full of workers, Poppeus had placed all of his family's silverware (118 pieces in all), jewels, and coins inside two wooden boxes and hidden them in an underground storage room.

At the time of the eruption, the freedman lived in a small apartment inside the house, perhaps with his young daughter. As the stones fell the first day, they filled the many open spaces of the house, trapping many people inside. By the time the stone fall had diminished on the second morning, almost everyone inside had decided to flee. Most were on their way upstairs, scaling the huge mounds of pumice, when the fourth surge hit them.

During the excavation of the house between 1926 and 1932, four different clusters of victims were found. The largest group consisted of ten people, one holding a lantern, near the staircase atop the pumice fall. On the top floor of the house, two women and a young girl were killed as they tried to reach the upper part of the stable to make their escape. A third group of three people was trapped inside a room on the first floor. In desperation, they used a pickax and a hoe to make a hole in the wall, trying to reach the others.

But perhaps the saddest discoveries were the skeletons of the freedman and the young girl who may have been his daughter. He had lain down on his bed and covered himself. Perhaps he was still asleep, or perhaps he resisted leaving the house of his employer. His daughter was at the foot of the bed when the surge hit.

House of Orpheus

Finally, another guard stood sentry in a nearby house, the House of Orpheus. Chained to his post, a watchdog was left in charge of this house. As the pumice fell, the dog climbed up and up as the stones accumulated. Eventually, the dog ran out of chain and was suffocated by the ash and pumice in an agonizing death well before the fourth surge occurred.

The skeleton of a baby was found inside the House of the Mosaic Atrium. The pyroclastic flow caused the floor of the house to buckle.

CHAPTER FIVE

HERCVLANEVM'S FATE

In 1929 laborers in Herculaneum used rail carts to speed the process of excavation.

Nine miles from Pompeii and only seven miles from Vesuvius, the town of Herculaneum, named after the Greek god Hercules, was subjected to the same eruption but with much different results. Because the volcanic cloud was blown away from Herculaneum, the town received only an inch or two of pumice. As a result, most of the residents were able to escape.

However, Herculaneum was destroyed during the second phase of the eruption. Unlike Pompeii, which experienced only the final three surges, Herculaneum was hit by all six, which included a much larger pyroclastic flow than at Pompeii. The first surge at 1:00 AM easily reached Herculaneum, killing anyone who remained there with the intensity of its heat. Accompanied by a minimal ash fall, it also turned wood into charcoal and ripped tiles from roofs. Soon after, the flow arrived: an oozing mud-like liquid filled with volcanic material (such as pumice and ash) and building material (such as tiles, bricks, and wood). By the time the other five surges had hit, Herculaneum was buried under more than sixty-five feet of volcanic deposits. In fact, there was so much volcanic debris that its shoreline on the Bay of Naples was pushed out at least another four hundred feet.

Because the amount of ash that accompanied the surge was minimal in Herculaneum, bodies of the victims were not completely covered the way they had been in Pompeii. This meant that they did not create molds inside the volcanic debris. What's more, until 1980, excavators had found only about a dozen skeletons at Herculaneum. Scientists assumed that most of the residents were able to leave, since the town hadn't been bombarded with pumice and rocks.

Three of these skeletons even have their own mysteries.

A skeleton of a teenage boy was found in a small bedroom inside the Gemstone Worker's shop. The bones allowed scientists to identify him as a teenager, but they concluded that he must have been sick, for his bones were small for his age. He had eaten a meal of chicken and discarded the bones in a bowl. As the surge approached, he must have become alarmed, for he hid his head under the bed. That was where he died. But why, scientists wondered, had he remained behind in his bedroom? Why hadn't he gone with someone when they fled

An archaeologist carefully removes the debris that encases this Roman soldier who died face-down on the beach at Herculaneum. Notice the sword that lies beside his right leg.

from the town? Had his parents run outside when Vesuvius began to erupt? If so, why hadn't they returned to get their son?

Similarly, in the House of the Mosaic Atrium, the remains of a baby were found in a crib. No other skeletons were found in the same house or in the streets outside. Did the parents leave the baby behind, or did something call them away, something from which they couldn't return?

The third mysterious skeleton belonged to a man found lying face-down on a bed in a room of the house called the Shrine of the Augustus. What puzzled scientists is that the door to the room was locked from the outside. Was he some type of criminal? they wondered.

In the 1980s, everything changed at Herculaneum when archaeologists began to excavate the site of the original shoreline. There they discovered more than three hundred skeletons along the ancient sea front. Scientists realized that many of Herculaneum's residents had tried to escape by sea. The people who had collected on the shore in the early morning hours had brought their valuables with them, perhaps waiting for the ideal time to depart.

Ring Lady was found on the beach wearing two rings and carrying other golden jewelry.

Some of the people died on the beach. One lady, now called the Ring Lady, was a tall, wealthy forty-five-year-old woman. The anthropologist who studied her bones found that she was a healthy woman who, though she had good teeth, suffered from gum disease. When the first surge hit, the Ring Lady was blown down on the sand and died immediately. She has become known for her beautiful jewelry: she wore two rings and carried two weighty snakehead bracelets and two earrings. All were made from gold.

Another skeleton found on the beach belonged to a soldier. He had fallen on his face when the surge blew through the town, as if he had been hit on the head and collapsed. However, the blast from the surge was so powerful that every bone in his body was broken except for those of his inner ear. He wore a sword and carried some coins. Nearby, perhaps carried on his back, was a set of carpenter's tools. His bones revealed that he was thirty-seven years old and had seen his share of fighting. Three teeth had been knocked out, and he had once been stabbed in the thigh. The weapon had gone so deep that it had penetrated his bone and left a scar.

The majority of the victims died as they huddled inside twelve vaulted boat sheds, or arcades, facing the beach. A group of twelve skeletons found in one shed told a moving

These are some of the twelve boat sheds that lined the shoreline at Herculaneum and provided momentary shelter for almost 300 people. The eruption extended the coastline by 400 feet.

story. According to the anthropologist Sara Bisel, this was a family and its slaves. The twelve people included three men, three women, a teenage girl, four children, and a baby. Of interest to Dr. Bisel was the teenage girl, who tightly clasped the baby in her arms. By studying the skeleton of the teenager, she could tell that the girl had had a hard life. Her teeth provided evidence that she had been malnourished when she was eleven months old. Her scarred arm bones showed that, although she was only fourteen, the girl had lifted amounts much too heavy for her. Dr. Bisel concluded that the girl was a slave, in charge of caring for the baby of a wealthy family.

Surprisingly, the people on the beach and the people in the arcades died different deaths. People on the beach died much more violently, as they were hit by the intensity of the first surge. Their bodies were blown to the ground; all of their skeletons were found in sprawled positions. At the same time, the tremendous heat (perhaps as high as 750 degrees Fahrenheit) essentially vaporized them. Their blood and bodily fluids boiled and evaporated; the skulls of some exploded and their bones were blackened. Death from the heat would have been instantaneous; they wouldn't have had a chance to take even one more breath.

On the other hand, people who had taken shelter in the boat arcades missed the impact of the violent surge. They were far from lucky, though, since they went into a kind of immediate, and deadly, heat shock. In two-tenths of a second, the flesh was seared from their bodies down to the bone. Because their bodies missed the surge blast, the skeletons looked quite different from the ones from the beach. Their feet and hand bones were contorted into odd positions as their bodies involuntarily reacted to the intense temperature.

Cracks in their teeth indicated that the temperature in the confined arcades rose to over 900 degrees Fahrenheit.

The people in the arcades would have been killed moments after those on the beach. They would have known that some type of tragedy was about to happen, from the rumble of the surge and the shaking of the earth. They might have looked toward the opening of the arcade for a moment, but most were found with their faces toward the rear of the arcades. Only a few brave souls had looked toward the opening at the time that the surge hit.

All were buried.

These people died in one of the arcades, or boat sheds, along the beachfront at Herculaneum. Sometimes replicas of the gruesome discoveries are exhibited in museums.

A look into the crater of Vesuvius on a foggy day may suggest that the volcano is extinct, but scientists know that it is only resting. Some consider Vesuvius the world's most dangerous volcano, because one million people live in its immediate vicinity.

CHAPTER SIX

A FINAL EXCAVATION

A transparent resin was used to capture the death of a teenage girl at a villa in Oplontis, an area outside Pompeii.

During the years that the plaster casts have been made at Pompeii, only one change has ever occurred in the technique used by archaeologists.

In 1984, on the outskirts of Pompeii, excavators found a villa where perhaps seventy-four victims had taken refuge from Vesuvius. As the first surge rolled over the villa around 1:00 AM, the people crowded toward the center of a room. Some died immediately from the heat and gas, but others survived a few moments more, long enough to move toward the door, climbing as they did on the bodies of those who had already died. Then the roof collapsed, killing everyone else.

Excavators of this villa were unable to create any plaster casts of the victims, with one exception. They came across a cavity where a young girl had been covered by ash. Instead of pouring plaster into the hollow space, however, they experimented by pouring wax into the cavity this time. Then they encased the wax form in plaster. Afterward, they melted the wax and poured it out, leaving a plaster mold with even more detail than a typical plaster cast. Finally, they filled the plaster mold with a resin that, when dried, would be transparent.

The final outcome was a lifelike and disturbing cast that shows the skeleton of the girl as well as the objects she was holding or wearing—in her case, a ring, an armband, and a hairpin. It also revealed all too clearly her agonized expression as she died.

Today Pompeii is a busy place, both as an archaeological site and as an adjacent modern town. More than two million people come to the ruins at Pompeii each year, many to see the body casts that Fiorelli began almost 150 years ago. Sometimes special exhibits are held

School and tourist groups regularly visit the plaster bodies displayed at Pompeii. These two bodies are exhibited in the macellum, a market area in Pompeii.

in museums to display the various discoveries from Pompeii. These include the beautiful artifacts and frescoes (that is, wall paintings) that archaeologists unearthed there, along with the heart-rending molds of bodies that have been made.

But Pompeii is in danger. Placed on the World Monuments Fund's list of endangered sites numerous times in recent years, the ruins of Pompeii are literally falling apart. Although about one-third of the site is still unexcavated, little funding is available for further excavation. Instead, archaeologists are much more concerned with repairing and restoring the buildings that have already been discovered. Many of the buildings that were uncovered early in the excavations have deteriorated from the constant exposure to the elements. Without second stories or roofs, these houses are especially unprotected from rain, which pools on the floor of many buildings and causes plaster walls to crack and sometimes collapse.

This farmer's field lies atop a large area of unexcavated ruins at Pompeii.

Even the plaster casts have not fared well. Over time, some have deteriorated, revealing the bones underneath. So many have been made that Pompeii does not even have a way to display most of them. Instead many are simply stored. Today, over a dozen can be found in a dark room, hidden behind bars, near the House of Menander. A few have been placed on shelves in the warehouse near the Forum. Even the ones that are on display are entombed in glass cases covered with grime.

When excavations at Pompeii are continued one day, archaeologists expect to find further cavities in the hardened deposits. They estimate that some five hundred more victims will be found when the rest of Pompeii is unearthed.

So many casts of bodies have been made that some are simply stacked on shelves in an open warehouse area near the Forum of Pompeii.

Today the guard dog from the House of Orpheus is stored in a warehouse, surrounded by other artifacts.

In the meantime, Vesuvius itself also remains a threat, not only to Pompeii but to the one million people who live in its vicinity today. Still considered a deadly volcano because a sudden pyroclastic eruption would affect so many more people, Vesuvius is carefully monitored for any signs of activity. If frequent earthquakes begin to rumble through the area or if any changes to the volcano's crater occur, authorities would began to evacuate anyone living close to Vesuvius. Whether that could be accomplished before an eruption occurred is something that officials don't know.

Until such a time, visitors can still climb to the top of Vesuvius and peer into its quiet crater. When Vesuvius isn't clouded over, they can even see all the way to the ruins of Pompeii and wonder what would happen if the volcano ever awakened again.

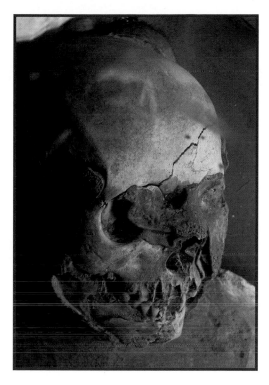

The plaster on some casts has deteriorated over time.

On a recent sunny summer's day, Vesuvius towers over the ruins of Pompeii. Scientists are concerned that another eruption may occur at any time.

ARCHAEOLOGICAL DIG SITES IN POMPEII

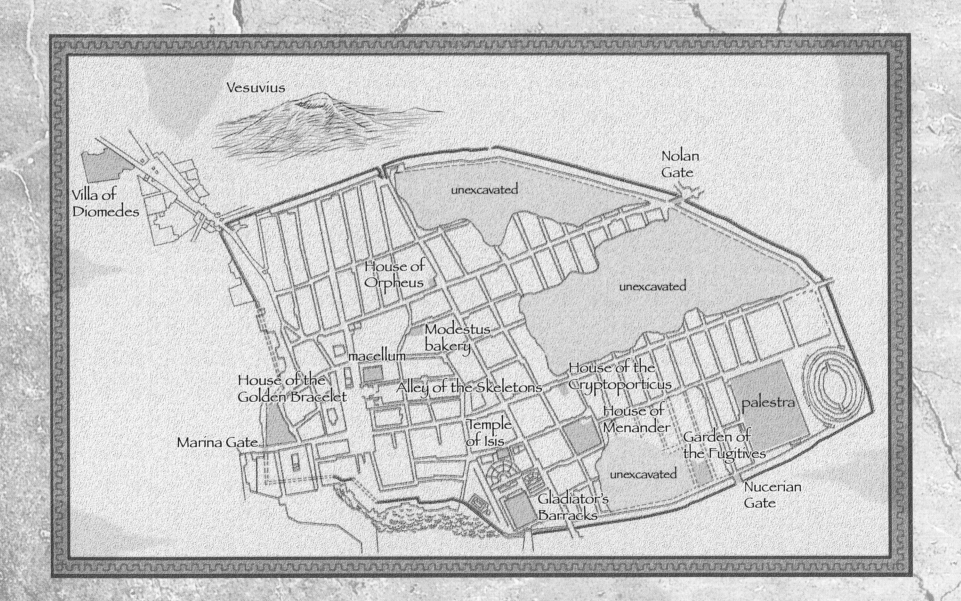

Vesuvius

Villa of Diomedes

Nolan Gate

unexcavated

unexcavated

House of Orpheus

Modestus bakery

macellum

House of the Cryptoporticus

House of the Golden Bracelet

Alley of the Skeletons

palestra

House of Menander

Temple of Isis

Garden of the Fugitives

Marina Gate

unexcavated

Gladiator's Barracks

Nucerian Gate

ACKNOWLEDGMENTS

Piecing together the story of the plaster bodies of Pompeii has been an archaeological excavation itself, and many people have assisted me, especially as I tried to ferret out rare photographic images.

I would like to thank Pier Giovanni Guzzo, archaeological superintendent of Pompeii, for allowing me to visit certain restricted buildings as well as the photography archive; Ida Mirra, of the press office of the Pompeii site, for her assistance; Valeria Sampaolo, archaeological superintendent for Naples and Caserta; and Alessandra Villone, director of the photo archive of the National Archaeology Museum of Naples, for their help in providing photographs used in this book.

Tim McCarthy of Artres.com also helped locate some long-lost Pompeii photos from the Alinari and Brogi archives. Tracey Schuster of the J. Paul Getty Museum in Los Angeles was very helpful in guiding me around the Getty's large photo archive of Pompeii material. Finally, gallery owner Ernst Bowinkel of Naples, Italy, allowed me to search his splendid collection of Pompeii material for just the right souvenirs to bring this book to life.

Amery, Colin, and Brian Curran Jr. *The Lost World of Pompeii*. Los Angeles: J. Paul Getty Museum, 2002.

Bahn, Paul G., ed. *The Cambridge Illustrated History of Archaeology*. Cambridge and New York: Cambridge University Press, 1996.

Barbet, Alix. *Les cités enfouies du Vésuve: Pompéi, Herculanum, Stabies et autres lieux*. Paris: Fayard, 1999.

Berry, Joanne, ed. *Unpeeling Pompeii: Studies in Region I of Pompeii*. Milan: Electa, 1998.

Bisel, Sara. *The Secrets of Vesuvius*. New York: Scholastic, 1990.

Bosch, Xavier. "Scientists Solve Mystery of Volcano's 'Natural Deaths.'" *British Medical Journal* 322 (April 2001): 946.

Cantarella, Eva, and Luciana Jacobelli. *A Day in Pompeii: Daily Life, Culture, and Society*. Naples: Electa Napoli, 2003.

Capasso, Luigi. "Herculaneum Victims of the Volcanic Eruptions of Vesuvius in 79 AD." *Lancet* 356 (November 2000): 1344–46.

Ciarallo, Annamaria, and Ernesto DeCarolis, eds. *Around the Walls of Pompeii: The Ancient City in Its Natural Environment*. Milan: Electa, 1998.

Cooley, Alison E. *Pompeii*. London: Duckworth, 2003.

Cooley, Alison, and M.G.L. Cooley. *Pompeii: A Sourcebook*. London: Routledge, 2004.

De Carolis, Ernesto. *Pompeii: A Reasoned Archaeological Itinerary*. Torre del Greco, Italy: T&M, 2001.

De Carolis, Ernesto, and Giovanni Patricelli. *Vesuvius A.D. 79: The Destruction of Pompeii and Herculaneum*. Los Angeles: J. Paul Getty Museum, 2003.

Deiss, Joseph Jay. *The Town of Hercules: A Buried Treasure Trove*. Rev. ed. Malibu, Calif.: J. Paul Getty Museum, 1995.

Etienne, Robert. *Pompeii: The Day a City Died*. New York: Abrams, 1992.

Gore, Rick. "The Dead Do Tell Tales at Vesuvius." *National Geographic* (May 1984): 557–613.

Guzzo, Pier Giovanni, and Antonio d'Ambrosio. *Pompeii: Guide to the Site*. Naples: Electa Napoli, 2002.

Guzzo, Pier Giovanni. *Pompeii: Ercolano, Stabiae, Oplontis: The Cities Buried by Vesuvius*. Naples: Electa Napoli, 2003.

———, ed. *Tales from an Eruption: Pompeii, Herculaneum, Oplontis; Guide to the Exhibition*. Milan: Electa, 2003.

Jacobelli, Luciana. *Gladiators at Pompeii*. Los Angeles: J. Paul Getty Museum, 2003.

Jenkins, Sid. "Pompeii Debris Yields Calamity Clues." *Science News* (March 13, 2004): 174.

Judge, Joseph. "On the Slope of Vesuvius: A Buried Roman Town Gives Up Its Dead." *National Geographic* (December 1982): 686–93.

Lessing, Erich, and Antonio Varone. *Pompeii*. Paris: Terrail, 2001.

Maiuri, Amedeo. "Last Moments of Pompeians." *National Geographic* (November 1961): 650–67.

———. *Pompeii*. Novara, Italy: Istituto Geografico de Agostini, 1963.

Mastrolorenzo, Giuseppe, et al. "Herculaneum Victims of Vesuvius in AD 79." *Nature* (April 12, 2001): 769–70.

New York Times. "Victims of Pompeii." November 17, 1882, 2.

Pellegrino, Charles. *Ghosts of Vesuvius: A New Look at the Last Days of Pompeii, How Towers Fall, and Other Strange Connections*. New York: Morrow, 2004.

Stefani, Grete, ed. *Menander: La Casa del Menandro di Pompei*. Milan: Electa, 2003.

Wallace, Jennifer. *Digging the Dirt: The Archaeological Imagination*. London: Duckworth, 2004.

Wilkinson, Paul. *Pompeii: The Last Day*. London: BBC Books, 2003.

Zanker, Paul. *Pompeii: Public and Private Life*. Translated by Deborah Lucas Schneider. Cambridge: Harvard University Press, 1998.